Journey to 31

A ROAD TO DISCOVERY

KENDRAMIAH P.

WESTBOW
PRESS®
A DIVISION OF THOMAS NELSON
& ZONDERVAN

WestBow Press books may be ordered through booksellers or by contacting:

WestBow Press
A Division of Thomas Nelson & Zondervan
1663 Liberty Drive
Bloomington, IN 47403
www.westbowpress.com
1 (866) 928-1240

ISBN: 978-1-9736-8483-1 (sc)
ISBN: 978-1-9736-8482-4 (e)

Print information available on the last page.

WestBow Press rev. date: 4/29/2020

Contents

Dedication

This book is dedicated to my beloved sister
Jackie for putting me in position.
May you rest in peace, my beautiful butterfly.

Epigraph

To all who have a dream and are hanging on by
a hope and a wish, Adonai will help you hold on
tighter and not let go. Truth, love, peace to you.

—Kendramiah P.

Foreword

Zuri Insikazi (My Mother)
Zuri (means *beautiful* in Swahili)
Insikazi (means *woman* Zulu)

As I have read my daughter's book in its entirety, I couldn't help taking a trip back down memory lane—the lane that I was in when God revealed to me that one of my children would one day spread his Word. I placed the gift on my youngest child because he was the one that people had given up on before they had given him a chance.

The saying goes, "God will use the least expected to spread his word." Today the revelation is clear. God has called my daughter, Miss Kendramiah. She was "the least expected" one. However, she is smart, went to college, and got a double degree. She is considered the quiet one, the one who is strong willed, the one who is no nonsense, the one who is a self-taught artist and photographer, and the one whom family members hold in high regard because of her accomplishments. Accolades from the world are great, however, all God wants her to be willing to do is spread His word in love, faith, and truth.

Lord God, I am pleased. I thank you for trusting me to be a vessel and to bring forth a child that would hear from you and answer your call. The world attests that there is no greater love than the love of a mother for her child. Lord God, I attest that you are the greatest lover of all. In spite of ourselves, you love us unconditionally. Lord, you are an awesome God. I praise you, honor you, thank you, and trust in you, in Jesus's name, amen.

And they, whether they will hear, or whether they will forbear, (for they are a rebellious house,) yet shall know that there hath been a prophet among them. (Ezekiel 2:5)

Heavenly Prayer

Dear Heavenly Father,

I humbly come before you and ask you to forgive my sins, whether they are known or unknown. I am still a sinner, but daily, you make me new.

Thank you, Adonai, for blessings that are known and unknown. Thank you for life and its many trials, tribulations, and creations, which have manifested in this work of art.

Thank you, Adonai, for molding and equipping me to be a soldier in the army of the Lord. Thank you, Heavenly Father, for the helmet of salvation, which kept me in my right mind enough so that I knew not to give up and to seek you daily. Thank you for the breastplate of righteousness, which covered my heart and increases the love I have for you, Adonai.

Thank you for the belt of truth that allowed me to hear your voice in the darkness. Thank you, Jesus, for fitting my feet with the readiness that comes from the gospel of peace. In times of turmoil, you allowed me to be *still*. Thank you for the shield of faith, which guards me against the spirit of doubt, confusion and envy and any iniquity that keeps me from you, Lord.

Hallelujah, Jesus. Lord, more than anything, thank you for the sword of the Spirit, which is your Word, God. For without it, even in my most vulnerable moments, I would have been defeated.

God, I give you all the glory, all the honor, and all the praise, in Jesus's name, amen.

Introduction

Thank you for taking the time to share this space of quiet time with your Lord and Savior, Jesus Christ. As you read and meditate on the words given, do not lean on your own understanding, but allow God the time to reveal what he has for you. I ask the Holy Spirit to come into your mind and to reveal new things in you.

Take your time while reading this book and don't feel pressured to finish a chapter a day. Be patient with yourself. Feel free to read the book in any order your spirit is leading you, for your everyday battles will not present themselves in the order that this book is written. If you are led to read a specific chapter to accommodate where you are in that moment, please do so.

Mark the pages and allow this to become personal for you. Our Heavenly Father loves it when we pursue a relationship with him.

In case no one has told you this, I love you! Life gets better if you will put it in the Master's hand.

The lined pages are provided for you to reflect. I usually write letters to God as a reflection about how I am really feeling. I've gained so much clarity through this, and I hope you will as well.

1

Run Your Race

*And let us not be weary in well doing: for in
due season we shall reap, if we faint not.
(Galatians 6:9)*

On this journey called life, we all have a part to play in helping one another. We are not meant to make this journey alone. The assignment the Lord gives you is meant for you to fulfill. In life, people are looking for wisdom and understanding on how to succeed, whether that be in career, family, or relationships, so that he or she may run the race with the full hope that it can be done. Life requires teamwork, no matter where you are or what you are doing.

For example, when a track team runs a relay race, the second person cannot run the race until the first person does. The first person has to run his or her segment of the race, no matter how short or long the distance is, and then pass the baton. It's about getting the job done. Runners must keep in mind that there is a third and a fourth runner waiting on them so that their team can win the race.

If you stop and give up in the beginning, you're being selfish toward the ones who are waiting on you. They can't finish a race that you ended in the beginning. So I tell you, run your race. Your peers have hope. Your children are looking up to you. Future generations depend on you to get it done.

Remain moral in all you do, and keep the Lord, Yeshua, first. Future generations are also watching to see if you have to cheat to win the race. They watch every detail and mimic what you do because you made it! Run your race because it's not about you, it's about who's behind you. Amen.

2

Victory in Jesus Christ

Many a time have they afflicted me from my youth, may
Israel now say: Many a time have they afflicted me from
my youth: yet they have not prevailed against me. The
plowers plowed upon my back: they made long their furrows.
The Lord is righteous: he hath cut asunder the cords of the
wicked. Let them all be confounded and turned back that
hate Zion. Let them be as the grass upon the housetops,
which withereth afore it groweth up: Wherewith the mower
filleth not his hand; nor he that bindeth sheaves his bosom.
Neither do they which go by say, The blessing of the Lord
be upon you: we bless you in the name of the Lord.
(Psalm 129:1–8)

Before the journey begins, know that the victory over the enemy has already been won. As you walk, know and understand that the work of the Lord is being manifested in your life daily.

Pray without ceasing. The enemy will try to capitalize on the trials and tribulations the Lord allows your way. Some days, the work of the Lord will hurt and even seem unbearable. Those around you will question your walk. Friends and family members will question the visions the Lord has given you. They will question your belief. You will face much hesitance, resistance, conviction, condemnation, betrayal, and judgement, but God will keep you.

Psalm 91:11 says, "For he shall give his angels charge over thee, to keep thee in all thy ways." Know that when you are in the will of God, not everyone will understand. The Lord loves you enough to surround you with people who do understand.

Pray for those who are against you. Pray that they will turn their hearts to the Lord for understanding. Mark 7:6 states, "He answered and said unto them, Well hath Esaias prophesied of you hypocrites, as it is written, This people honoureth me with their lips, but their heart is far from me."

The Lord is intentional in all he does. Amen.

3

Harden Not Your Heart

But whosoever shall deny me before men, him will I
also deny before my Father which is in heaven.
(Matthew 10:33)

When your heart becomes hard like bricks toward others, it also becomes hard like bricks toward God. He needs to get in. Soften your heart and let God in. If a song of worship makes you cry, cry. The Lord is trying to get in and heal you. Let Him in. He needs you for his kingdom. He has an anointing on your life that he needs to show you. He has a greater use for you than you do for yourself.

When you are in pain from life's journey, feel the pain but don't stay there. Allow yourself to feel the emotion and as you do, call on the name of Jesus, Yeshua, to consume you. Call on the Holy Spirit to fill you. Cry out to Adonai to fill you where you are empty.

Ask your heavenly angels for help. They are beside you. They are waiting for you to say the word. In an emergency, you need to immediately call 911, and they may or may not show up. Dial your Heavenly Father, and he will show up *every* time, per Psalm 91:11. He is your 911. But he'll do more than rescue you. He'll make you new and whole again!

He loves you so much that he's calling you. He'll redial your number until you answer. The Lord knows you may not trust him, and he has forgiven you for that. But I'll tell you now, going down the path of unrighteousness leads to a dead end. Whomever this is for, God is calling you. Pick up the phone and live.

4

Drown Your Heart in Forgiveness

*And forgive us our debts, as we forgive
our debtors. (Matthew 6:12)*

Because we never know what someone else is going through or the reason why, along our journeys, we may run into many situations with our counterparts that we don't understand. With all the strength in us, we try to wrap our minds around the *why*.

I myself have been confused about situations, and years later, I still don't understand. I prayed day and night for the Lord to bring clarity so that my mind might be at ease. When I didn't know how to formulate my prayer the *proper* way to get the *right* answer, my prayer to the Lord would always be, "God, make it right."

The truth is—you won't get an answer for every situation. I've had to learn to rest in God. Although it is difficult, I've had to say, "Thank you, Jesus." I then began to give him thanks for delivering me from situations that could have been worse. I told him, "Thank you for saving me."

This is what we must understand about our Lord and Savior: He knows, hears, and sees *all*. He is at work on our behalves at all times.

So when he brings a situation to a halt, give him praise. When he changes the direction that you are going, give him praise. Through the pain, give him praise. Through the heartache, give him praise. Through the tears, give him praise. James 1:2–3 says, "My brethren, count it all joy when ye fall into divers' temptations; Knowing this, that the trying of your faith worketh patience."

Know and understand that everyone has a spiritual battle of some sort that he or she does not even understand. At times, that person's response to you might not even be a reflection of him or her but of the battle against the enemy within. Step away and give it all to God. Let God do his part. All the Lord asks you to do is forgive and move on. Amen.

5

Take Up Your Cross

The increase from the land is taken by all;
the king himself profits from the fields.
(Ecclesiastes 5:9 NIV)

God the Creator profits greatly when a soul is saved and is brought into the kingdom. As I began to write this chapter, the Lord gave me the verse for this text, but I didn't understand it at first. Then the Lord revealed that you and I are treasures to Christ. You are worth more than the universe itself. You are precious in his sight and so is everyone else in the world.

No matter what your background is, he does not discriminate. He's waiting for you to commit your life to him. He's ready to show you just how much you mean to him.

First, you must deny your flesh and all earthly things and take up your cross. So many lies of the enemy have been whispered in your ear, and you have begun to believe them. God will no longer allow the whispers of unclean spirits to consume you and tell you that you are not worthy. Unrighteousness will no longer ring in your ears. Rededicate your life fully. Allow God to drain you of all your iniquities and make you clean again. He has something that he needs to tell you, but first, you must take up your cross. Amen.

6

Purposeful Pain

Many a time have they afflicted me from my youth, may Israel now say: Many a time have they afflicted me from my youth: yet they have not prevailed against me. The plowers plowed upon my back: they made long their furrows. The Lord is righteous: he hath cut asunder the cords of the wicked. Let them all be confounded and turned back that hate Zion. Let them be as the grass upon the housetops, which withereth afore it groweth up: Wherewith the mower filleth not his hand; nor he that bindeth sheaves his bosom. Neither do they which go by say, The blessing of the Lord be upon you: we bless you in the name of the Lord.
(Psalm 129:1–8)

Even while you were in the womb, the enemy saw you at your greatest. He saw the promises the Lord had in store for you. From your youth, he began to attack you. The pain you are experiencing is birthing purpose. Every trial and tribulation is intentional on the Lord's behalf. Even when you stray outside of his will, he will give that choice a purpose.

Romans 8:28 states, "And we know that all things work together for good to them that love God, to them who are the called according to his purpose." No matter how far you go, no matter how long it takes you to get back, and no matter what you did, Yeshua will not let it be in vain.

When guilt and shame try to invade your prayer and meditation time, with kingdom authority, you evict them from your holy space. The Spirit of Christ lives within you and consumes you, leaving no room for the enemy. God needs every ounce of you. Every wrinkle on your body and hair on your head belongs to Yeshua. There is no vacancy ever. Don't even allow the lies of the enemy to make a reservation at the temple. The Lord needs to reveal your purpose to you.

I tell you, live. Through trials and tribulations, live. On your good days, live. On gloomy days, live. Just live and pray. Amen.

7

Let's Talk Business

So I was great, and increased more than all that were before me in Jerusalem: also my wisdom remained with me.
(Ecclesiastes 2:9)

God honors purpose that honors him. What is your why, your motivation? What makes you go after your goals? Does your why help build the kingdom of glory? The pain you are experiencing is birthing your purpose.

When I quit my job as a data analyst, it caused a bit of chaos in my world. My parents were happy but unsure at the same time. I quit a full-time job to go part-time, based purely on faith. I wasn't happy anymore. I didn't feel I was honoring the Lord completely with my work. Yes, I was making a great impact in the workplace and in my community, but my heart knew there was more inside me that I needed to discover. I was ready to be used by God.

Before the transition was made, I asked the Lord for help. A friend told me about the prayer of Jabez and how the Lord heard his cry and answered it. In 1 Chronicles 4:10, it says, "And Jabez called on the God of Israel, saying, 'Oh that thou wouldest bless me indeed, and enlarge my coast, and that thine hand might be with me, and that thou wouldest keep me from evil, that it may not grieve me! And God granted him that which he requested."

By the way, I have read this scripture many times but never before received the revelation that the Lord just gave me as I was typing this. The Holy Spirit prompted a question to me. "What will you do when your name is called?" This particular part of 1 Chronicles is naming Judah's descendants. The Lord correlated it to a roll call for me. When a teacher calls your name, you answer with "here" or "present." When Jabez's name was called, he had something to say to the Lord. He had a request.

What will you do when your name is called? I asked the

Lord what I should do. I was ready for something new. The job offered a lot of stability, but at that moment, I felt suffocated and just needed God. I was afraid I wouldn't find another job. I thought leaving would be the biggest mistake I could make. Deep down, a part of me knew that when I left my current job, there was more in store for me. But it required me to give up what was comfortable.

The hardest part of the battle was trusting God's Word. He said that he would never leave me or forsake me. After fasting, I finally mustered up the spiritual strength to put in my two weeks' notice. Keep in mind that I had known that I needed to take this step about a year or so before this moment, but I had ignored it. I had not understood how much the Lord loved me and that when he said he was going to do something, he meant it.

I remember sitting with my mom. I was in tears about what was going on because she couldn't understand why God would want me to quit a full-time job to go part time. She just kept asking, "What are you doing? What's your plan?" I had no answers. All I had was the word of the Lord. All I knew was that I wanted to travel the world and change people's lives.

When I told her this, she asked me, "So what do you call what you're doing?" I was stumped. I went to work the next day while really contemplating the question. Then it just hit me. I thought, *I'm a philanthropist.* Then I had to ask myself, *Why do I want to be blessed with something else?* My answer was, *I want to change the lives of our youth. They are my why.* Then the windows of heaven opened up.

Of course, I went home full of excitement and told my mom that the revelation had shown me there was nothing wrong with making a request to the Lord. He would still bless me. But to experience the *full* blessings of the Lord—not only financially but in wisdom and healthier relationships—my why had to serve the Lord and his kingdom.

We must be about the kingdom's business. Amen.

8

God Is

*The Lord is my shepherd; I shall not want. He maketh me
to lie down in green pastures: he leadeth me beside the still
waters. He restoreth my soul: he leadeth me in the paths of
righteousness for his name's sake. Yea though I walk through
the valley of the shadow of death, I will fear no evil: for thou
art with me, thy rod and thy staff they comfort me. Thou
preparest a table before me in the presence of mine enemies:
thou anointest my head with oil; my cup runneth over.
Surely goodness and mercy shall follow me all the days of
my life: and I will dwell in the house of the Lord forever.*

(Psalm 23)

Throughout my journey, I have lacked nothing. I have always had a place to stay, food to eat, and clothes on my back. This is the Lord's promise to you and me. He is our provider.

There were days when the stress wreaked havoc in my heart and mind. Many days, I didn't know whose voice was speaking to me. Was it God's voice or my adversary's voice?

It's intriguing, I know. As you walk with Christ, the opposition will try to throw everything that it can at you, to push you outside of the Lord's will. It can't do anything but talk.

A good friend of mine told me the enemy (unclean spirits) couldn't take my blessings from me. He could only try to persuade me to walk away from them or throw them away. He couldn't push me outside of the Lord's will. His objective was to get me to step outside of the Lord's protection and will for my life. I thank God for His protection over the attack of the enemy. Yeshua is my protector.

Hearing clearly from the Lord was hard for me at times. I started to encounter people with prophetic spiritual gifts, which was new for me. As a believer, you can become caught up in depending heavily on a word from a prophet or prophetess. I didn't depend on their words, but some days, I found myself so out of order that I needed someone to give me a word from the Lord.

One day, God made his presence known even more to me. I was standing in church praising at the altar, and then I felt a presence like a rushing wind. I felt the presence of the Creator Adonai. Yahweh himself prophesied to me so that I would begin to trust him even more and no longer seek a word from someone else. I no longer needed a prophet or prophetess to tell me what the Lord could come and tell me directly. God is my teacher and guide.

9

Say Thank You

*I will lift up mine eyes unto the hills, from whence cometh
my help. My help cometh from the Lord, which made
heaven and earth. He will not suffer thy foot to be moved:
he that keepeth thee will not slumber. Behold, he that
keepeth Israel shall neither slumber nor sleep. The Lord is
thy keeper: the Lord is thy shade upon thy right hand. The
sun shall not smite thee by day, nor the moon by night.
The Lord shall preserve thee from all evil: he shall preserve
thy soul. The Lord shall preserve thy going out and thy
coming in from this time forth, and even for evermore.*

(Psalm 121:1–8)

A simple thank-you is all that the Lord requires of us on a daily basis. He does so much for us when we are asleep and awake. Whether we know it or not, he is always at work on our behalves. He does not have to discuss what he is doing with us. He simply gets it done. Even though we fail him daily, he still loves us enough to forgive us and bless us beyond what we deserve. Learn how to say thank you more. He is a simple God. Don't make Him complicated. It's as simple as that. Amen.

10

Happy Birthday

Where there is no vision, the people perish: but
he that keepeth the law, happy is he.
(Proverbs 29:18)

As the clock struck 12:00 a.m., I sat in the dark on the floor of my room and reflected on my twenty-eighth year. I tried to figure out what I had really done. For a few seconds, I felt like a failure and as if I hadn't accomplished anything. I didn't have children. I wasn't married. I was not working at a big-time corporation making huge bucks and traveling the world.

In that same instance, I was given a reality check from the Lord. I saw an endless vision. The journey I had been on those past few months had allowed the Lord to show me who I was in him and not who I was in the world. Each time I had gotten down to my last bit of energy to keep going and had just known that I was going to give up, the Lord had picked me up and had instilled more of his strength in me. When it had come to a point where I had no more fight in me, my last option had been to draw on the strength of Yahweh himself. Each time had been a moment of growth. I had broken through another layer of who I was not, so that he could reveal who I am.

Joy began to consume my soul, because the Lord revealed that the greatest gift I could receive directly from the Creator was vision—not just any type of vision, but endless vision. Not only did I know who and whose I was, but also my purpose. I should never again question Yahweh on what I needed to do for him. He had stored up so many ideas and projects, that I would be unpacking them for the rest of my life.

Psalm 136:1 tells us to give thanks to the Lord, for he is good. His love endures forever. My heart is full of gratitude because of the gift of *vision*. The best gift from the Creator is endless vision.

"But I rejoiced in the Lord greatly, that now at the last your care of me hath flourished again; wherein ye were also careful, but ye lacked opportunity." (Philippians 4:10)

11

Love God

Love not the world, neither the things that are in the world. If any man love the world, the love of the Father is not in him. For all that is in the world, the lust of the flesh, and the lust of the eyes, and the pride of life, is not of the Father, but is of the world. And the world passeth away, and the lust thereof: but he that doeth the will of God abideth for ever.

(1 John 2:15–17)

Until you love God, you can't truly love yourself. We've all had relationships that were not of God. We've all had relationships that the Lord ordained us to go through. We've all had relationships that have caused us at the end of the day, to wonder, what was that, or what happened? Because of the significant amount of love that we have for the world, we tend to get stuck there instead of continuing to walk with God.

Your emotions and feelings tell you that the person stole your heart or that he or she is the one that got away. You don't understand how that individual could do that. The biggest question I always asked was, what did I do wrong?

When I discovered who I was in God, I also released who I was in the world. Then the Lord began to reveal things to me. Yahweh revealed that when a person left me, that individual took something that wasn't mine to begin with. When I had the spirit of insecurity consuming me, someone would come along that path and reveal it, not so that it would consume me but so that I could give it to God. He would replace it with security in him.

Trials and tribulations come along to expose what is going on under the surface so that you will hand it over to God. He fills the void or the empty space with love to make you complete.

I use to chant all day, "Love yourself. Love yourself!" yet I was still living in sin, falling into the hands of the enemy, and letting his spirits consume me. That's when I learned that I was only halfway there. Yes, do love yourself, but how? Draw closer to God every time a situation happens so that he can complete you and fill you with the Holy Spirit. Stay covered. Love God first.

12

The Proverbs Thirty-One Man

*The words of king Lemuel, the prophecy that his mother taught
him. What, my son? and what, the son of my womb? and what, the
son of my vows? Give not thy strength unto women, nor thy ways
to that which destroyeth kings. It is not for kings, O Lemuel, it is
not for kings to drink wine; nor for princes strong drink: Lest they
drink, and forget the law, and pervert the judgment of any of the
afflicted. Give strong drink unto him that is ready to perish, and
wine unto those that be of heavy hearts. Let him drink, and forget
his poverty, and remember his misery no more. Open thy mouth for
the dumb in the cause of all such as are appointed to destruction.
Open thy mouth, judge righteously, and plead the cause of the
poor and needy. Who can find a virtuous woman? for her price
is far above rubies. The heart of her husband doth safely trust
in her, so that he shall have no need of spoil ... Her husband is
known in the gates, when he sitteth among the elders of the land.
(Proverbs 31:1–11, 23)*

I was dreaming that I was talking to my mom. She was telling me about how she was talking to the Lord. She was with her guy friend, and they heard the footsteps of the Lord behind them. They came out of a store, and when she walked and then paused, she heard them. When he walked and paused, he heard the footsteps too. When they both walked together, they both heard the footsteps of the Lord.

In the middle of her story, I heard her say, "Kendra," which got more of my attention. In the dream, hearing my name called made me think God was using my mom to get my attention. I know that when someone usually hears his or her name called like that, that person is supposed to answer, "Here I am Lord. Your faithful servant is listening." So after a few seconds, that's what I said. All I heard back was, "Walk," and it was as clear as day.

When you and the person you are pursuing walk with Christ, you will know because God is with you and he makes his presence known to the both of you. Your steps will be the same.

"Rooted and built up in him, and stablished in the faith, as ye have been taught, abounding therein with thanksgiving." (Colossians 2:7)

13

Don't Sprout Then Doubt

But they were terrified and affrighted, and supposed that they had seen a spirit. And he said unto them, Why are ye troubled? and why do thoughts arise in your hearts?
(Luke 24:37–38)

Let God do what he promised to do for you. When you get up in the morning, thank God for a fresh new opportunity.

Often, I can't believe what God has done for me and through me. Although he has been very consistent, I still can't believe that he can do it again. At times, it does not make sense that God has been able to answer all my prayers, big and small. What baffles me is that he keeps doing what he said he would do.

I grew and grew and then hit a moment of disbelief that I could ever grow again. I hit a moment of disbelief that God could turn my situation around. I hit a moment of disbelief that God could give me something better.

I'm growing through his Word as I seek him. I have grown exponentially in all areas of life yet still have moments when I ask, is this really happening? The answer is *yes!* Yes, he keeps his promises. Yes, he loves you no matter what. Yes, he blesses you despite the circumstances in front of you. Yes, he will allow good people to come into your life, who will love you no matter what. The answer is yes.

We doubt what we see. Why? It is because of fear. Fear can kill manifestations on a daily basis, if we let it. When the Lord says he's going to do something, believe it. The Lord's promises do not come back void. We must be in tune with him at all times to know what these promises are. We may want one thing, but God might want something else for us.

Learn, during this journey, to follow your heart. Put your heart in the hands of the Lord, and he will never leave you or forsake you. Along the way, the Lord will confirm his promises so that you will have the strength to get to the finish line. Know that even at the finish line, it is only the beginning of the next phase of promises.

The Lord is strengthening you in patience, peace, wisdom, courage, knowledge, and joy so that you can serve the Lord. Some things require more preparation time before you can receive them. As he walks and talks with you, acknowledge the prayers that he has already answered. They are proof that he has heard you and has not forgotten about you and the major thing you have trusted him to manifest. He hears you loud and clear every day. He loves you enough to prepare you at His pace and not your own.

Speak life into your circumstance and stand in agreement with Adonai regarding the promises for your life. Thank God. Continuing to worship and praise protects you against yourself. I thank God for pulling me out of that pit of fear and pushing me forward.

Drown yourself in *love*, *truth*, and *understanding*. Give it to God. Learn how to speak life and not death. Thank you, Jesus, for deliverance.

"Death and life are in the power of the tongue: and they that love it shall eat the fruit thereof." (Proverbs 18:21)

14

In Advance

*I will go before thee, and make the crooked
places straight: I will break in pieces the gates of
brass, and cut in sunder the bars of iron:
(Isaiah 45:2)*

Have you ever been in a situation that you wished would go away? You get into a disagreement with someone over an email or a text message. You know that you have to face that person eventually. You go over all the thoughts you're prepared to say to that individual. Your frustration won't allow you to understand that it's already been done. God has already taken care of it. So you rehash what you're going to say and how you're going to say it.

Maybe you have a bill that's late and don't know what you're going to tell the bill collectors. You're trying to decide whether to lie or to tell the truth. You have worked out in your mind what's going to happen. If they say something, you know what your response will be.

God has already gone ahead of you and fixed the situation. Your needs have already been met before you need something. It was in place years before you needed it. Not only is he an on-time God, but he is an already-there God.

15

Where You Are

*I will open rivers in high places, and fountains in
the midst of the valleys: I will make the wilderness a
pool of water, and the dry land springs of water.
(Isaiah 41:18)*

As I was reading this scripture, I understood that everybody is blessed. If you're sitting on the mountaintop of life, you are blessed. If you're stuck in a valley, you will be blessed. If you're lost, you will be blessed. If there's a drought where you live, you will be blessed. Whatever stage you are at in life you will be blessed.

First, give your life to Christ, and wherever you are when you decide this, he will bless you automatically. Place forgiveness in your heart, and he will give you grace and mercy. He is ready for his people to come back to him. Therefore, when you dedicate your life back to Christ wholeheartedly, heaven will rejoice and pour out *all* that has been stored up for you. As a matter of fact, the Lord loves you so much that heaven has descended to earth, and the angels are walking right beside you. The minute you tell God, "Tag, you're it!" he takes over. I'll say it for you, "God, tag, you're it!"

16

Apologize

*For this is the message that ye have heard from the
beginning, that we should love one another.
(1 John 3:11)*

Because God first loved you, apologies kill pride, guilt, and shame. The enemy feeds on the many apologies that go unspoken. You justify in your mind, over and over, why an apology is not necessary, yet you toss and turn at night with guilt. Guilt and pride sleep together, therefore, they manifest themselves in your bed and confuse your mind with justification, day in and day out.

They block the nudge you've been given to apologize. It's a small and gentle touch. In it, there is no condemnation but there is freedom. Guilt, pride, shame, and sin are spiritual infections that will *never* go away without a word from God. No one in your circle can give you a word of peace except God. As a matter of fact, these people could be the very things causing the disease to spread. Of course, they think they're helping by offering justification. Read the story of Job and see how far his friends and family got him. It was not until he heard a word from the Lord that he was set free.

"And they were calling to one another: "Holy, holy, holy is the Lord Almighty; the whole earth is full of his glory." At the sound of their voices the doorposts and thresholds shook and the temple was filled with smoke. "Woe to me!" I cried. "I am ruined! For I am a man of unclean lips, and I live among a people of unclean lips, and my eyes have seen the King, the Lord Almighty." Then one of the seraphim flew to me with a live coal in his hand, which he had taken with tongs from the altar. With it he touched my mouth and said, "See, this has touched your lips; your guilt is taken away and your sin atoned for." (Isaiah 6:3–7 NIV)

17

Who Takes the Credit?

Blessed is the man that walketh not in the counsel of the ungodly, nor standeth in the way of sinners, nor sitteth in the seat of the scornful. But his delight is in the law of the Lord; and in his law doth he meditate day and night. And he shall be like a tree planted by the rivers of water, that bringeth forth his fruit in his season; his leaf also shall not wither; and whatsoever he doeth shall prosper.
(Psalm 1:1–3)

I pray that whatever you're going through at this moment, you can give it all to God. Whether it is good or bad, give it to him.

Know that whenever things seem to turn upside down, it isn't always the enemy. The Lord has the power to make you uncomfortable, take another path, stop where you are, and revise some things. The difference is that the enemy wants to destroy you, but the Lord will make your enemy your footstool. The Lord wants to promote you and make you better. The road to better has valleys too.

What comes easily, goes away easy. What you work to get, you work to keep because you're constantly reminded of how hard you fought to get there. Whomever this is for, know that the Lord loves you with all his heart. He has not forgotten about you nor will he ever. My God, the Lord, is good. While typing this message, the Lord gave me Psalm 21:11, which says, "For they intended evil against thee: they imagined a mischievous device, which they are not able to perform. Therefore shalt thou make them turn their back, when thou shalt make ready thine arrows upon thy strings against the face of them. Be thou exalted, Lord, in thine own strength: so will we sing and praise thy power." (Psalm 21:11–13)

18

Pay Attention

*But blessed are your eyes because they see, and your ears
because they hear. For truly I tell you, many prophets and
righteous people longed to see what you see but did not
see it, and to hear what you hear but did not hear it.
(Matthew 13:16–17 NIV)*

Pay attention is one of the simplest instructions that the Lord can give you. He is always speaking. When you're in class and the teacher is telling you the answers to an upcoming test and giving you information of importance that will be needed later, are you listening?

Manifestations happen daily. Unless you are in tune with God, you won't see them. You'll constantly ask God, "Why aren't you doing anything? Why aren't you helping me?" The Lord always answers and moves on your behalf. When you get distracted, you won't hear what Jesus is saying.

Matthew 6:9-13, Jesus said, "Our father who art in heaven, hallowed be thy name. Thy kingdom come, thy will be done. On earth as it is in heaven. Give us this day our daily bread. Forgive us our debts, as we forgive our debtors and lead us not into temptation. But deliver us from the evil one. For thine is the kingdom and the power, and the glory forever," in Yeshua's name, amen. The Lord needs your undivided attention.

"But seek ye first the kingdom of God, and his righteousness; and all these things shall be added unto you." (Matthew 6:33)

19

I Love Your Presence

*Those things, which ye have both learned, and
received, and heard, and seen in me, do: and
the God of peace shall be with you.*
(Philippians 4:9)

Your journey and walk with Christ gets difficult when friends and family don't love Christ the way you do. It's not that you don't love or believe in God, but your frustration shows when you can't understand why your friends and family don't love him the way you do.

You trust and you believe in him. All you want is for those around you—the ones you talk to consistently—to love and trust him just as much as you do when you're going through something. That way, they're not looking at you and asking why and how. Instead, they simply and without hesitance go to Christ on your behalf for him to work it out. They thank him for what he is doing on your behalf. When they find themselves in your very position, they trust him enough to know that Christ is already at work because they've seen Him work in your life.

20

The Love of God Transcends All

I thank God for you. There are some days when you may not have the energy to read and meditate on a full passage. Therefore, I have provided scriptures for you to think about in their simplicity as God delivers the word he has specifically for you.

Jesus died for you. (John 3:16).

Adonai is our fortress. (Psalm 91:11)

There is healing in his dwelling place. (Psalm 119)

Seek ye first his kingdom. (Matthew 6:33)

He will make our path straight. (Proverbs 3:6)

He will open the windows of heaven. (Malachi 3:10)

He has given you vision. (Proverbs 29:18)

Have faith. (James 2:14–26 and Hebrews 11:1)

I love you forever. (John 15:9)

Be patient. (Philippians 4:6)

Remember what he has already done. (Philippians 4:9)

Think good thoughts. (Philippians 4:8)

Answer when you're called. (1 Chronicles 4:10)

21

Let Them Believe

Do you now believe? Jesus replied.
(John 16:31 NIV)

Your belief is the breadth that is needed for your desires to come to life. Many times, God showed me what he was going to do for me, and I believed him. When I shared *his* vision for me with others, I then started to doubt. Why did I do this? I doubted because they doubted. Don't allow this to happen to you. Take what God says, protect it, nurture it, love on it, speak life into it, and watch it blossom with the water of belief.

Here is an example. There was a time in my life when I was not working and trying to find a job was more difficult than paying bills with no money. I went to many job interviews. If I lumped all the responses that I received into one pile, it would be, "You wouldn't like it here. We can't afford you. You're better off freelancing." What was I to do with this? I went to God and asked, "What do I do?"

Then I had a thought. *What do I have?* I thought about it for a second and reminded myself of my accomplishments over the years: the degrees I had obtained, my years of experience in education, my drive for service, being an artist, my love of working with youth, being knowledgeable about technology, being an entrepreneur, and more than anything else, wanting to be obedient to God.

I was guided to create and to focus on my business. I did. Many people around me, including family, doubted what I was doing and why I was doing it. All I could tell them was that I had to be obedient.

Months later, I experienced the fruit of my labor of walking in obedience. The same people that doubted me are now supporting me 100 percent. Now please don't take this as one of those let-your-haters-be-your-motivators speeches. That is definitely not what this is. This is a speech about doing what God says to do so that those watching can be obedient and believe him when he does it for them.

Did I make you smile? I hope so. The best is yet to come.

22

God's Perspective

*We demolish arguments and every pretension that sets
itself up against the knowledge of God, and we take
captive every thought to make it obedient to Christ.
(2 Corinthians 10:5 NIV)*

Life is about perspective. So let me tell you a bit about perspective and the way it has helped me grow as a woman. The word says in 1 Corinthians 13:10–11, "But when that which is perfect has come, then that which is in part will be done away. When I was a child, I spoke as a child, I understood as a child, I thought as a child; but when I became a man, I put away childish things" (NKJV).

Let go of all that you thought you knew before you became one with Christ and the person they said you were or would be. What? I know, right? It's a harsh reality because the truth of the matter is that when you join forces with Almighty God, there is work to be done. There are spells (I mean bondage) to be broken. There are dark souls to light up. There are crooked paths to be made straight. There are seeds to bloom. There are hungry bellies to be fed. There are soulless people to breathe life into.

It's heavy, right? But this is God's perspective. Are we striving to be seen, or are we striving to give God all the glory? That makes all the difference as to whether or not we fall into depression after conquering an enemy and getting the victory. Why would we fall into depression? Sometimes, we do things that give us all the glory. Then we feel empty when it stops.

Perspective makes a big difference when your job is stressing you out. What you see as them piling work on you and making you overwork for minor pay is God preparing you. I had to say, "Hey! Stay grounded and focused and get your future company in order from bottom to top." You have to be faithful and content where He has placed you so that he can strategically move you.

Whoa! Remember, it's not all about you. It never is. You're just the vessel he decided to use for such an amazing task. Well, it's time to get some new glasses so that you will have twenty-twenty vision.

23

Stay in Position

Therefore put on the full armor of God, so that when the day of evil comes, you may be able to stand your ground, and after you have done everything, to stand.
(Ephesians 6:13 NIV)

When faced with the bread of adversity and the water of affliction, know that God is right beside you. Know in this moment that God is pressing you to grow. Jeremiah 17:8 states, "For he shall be as a tree planted by the waters, and that spreadeth out her roots by the river, and shall not see when heat cometh, but her leaf shall be green; and shall not be careful in the year of drought, neither shall cease from yielding fruit." One day, take some time to go outside and sit in front of a tree. When you look at this tree, ask yourself if it is moving. Observe the tree during a storm, when it rains, and when the sun is shining brightly. When the wind is blowing, what is the tree doing? It stays rooted. It allows the Lord to nurture and purify it so that it can continue to produce good fruit.

What am I saying? In all you do, be still. Much will come upon you to distract you and throw you off your course. Vulnerabilities are doors that get to you. Take some time to sit in the Lord's presence and ask him to help you identify your vulnerabilities. As you do so, put on the full armor of God so that you may stand in the face of adversity. Put on the full armor and stay in position.

24

Destination Determined

For we are God's handiwork, created in Christ Jesus to do good works, which God prepared in advance for us to do. (Ephesians 2:10 NIV)

Have you ever flown on a plane and pondered what your destination would be like? You might have already determined it in your mind or even created your itinerary for the trip's festivities. Do you trust God to do the same for you? Do you trust him to give you a destination and to create an itinerary for all that you will enjoy doing during your visit (assignment)? Each assignment in your life is a destination that has already been determined.

I've experienced much of God's blessings and anointing on my life when I've allowed Him to fly the plane and to direct me to my destination. Upon arrival, he gave me an itinerary. Much to my surprise, it was better than I had expected it to be.

When you are in the will of God, you surrender your itinerary. I heard someone say, "You will never truly arrive." The truth is that you will never arrive at a destination that God does not have planned for you. Surrender your itinerary.

25

Letting Go

We demolish arguments and every pretension that sets itself up against the knowledge of God, and we take captive every thought to make it obedient to Christ.
(2 Corinthians 10:5 NIV)

Letting go is the easiest thing to do with God's help. I faced an obstacle in life where I had a choice to remain in it or to put it down. Because of a revelation from God, I thought about the opportunity and all of the consequences that came with it. In that moment, I saw myself holding a glass filled with a dark liquid. I didn't pay much attention to the color of the liquid in that moment, but I saw myself put the glass on the table and walk away from it.

I was telling my friends how this opportunity no longer appealed to me once I had put it down. They asked me how I did it. I told them that I didn't know how but that I just did it.

I'm grateful to the Lord for showing me that I had strength within me that I didn't know existed. In that moment of needing to let go of something that would usually consume me, he took over and helped me. *He* told me, " 'My grace is sufficient for you, for my power is made perfect in weakness.' Therefore, I will boast all the more gladly about my weaknesses, so that Christ's power may rest on me." (2 Corinthians 12:9 NIV).

Honestly, letting go is tough, but it is easy when you allow God to assist you. You have to be willing to let it go. Put it down.

"Come to me, all you who are weary and burdened, and I will give you rest. Take my yoke upon you and learn from me, for I am gentle and humble in heart, and you will find rest for your souls. For my yoke is easy and my burden is light." (Matthew 11:28-30 NIV)

26

A Word from Papa

Grandchildren are the crown of the aged, and
the glory of children is their fathers.
(Proverbs 17:6 ESV)

"The world is waiting on you," my papa said as I sat with him one day. He has become like a best friend. He said this to me when I was trying to figure out my life—what I was going through and why. I sat there full of anxiety and depression. Everyone around me was asking me a million questions—questions I didn't have answers to. What was I to do? I heard what my papa said and let his words sink in. I wrote it down and meditated on it. It was one of the greatest things my papa could have said to me.

What am I saying? Although I was in a place of despair and was full of anxiety and depression, my Heavenly Father sent a word through my papa to tell me that the world was waiting on me. That meant God was not done with me yet. It was a seed that had been planted in my soul, which I was responsible for nurturing. What I saw as despair mixed with anxiety and depression was actually God planting me in soil so that He could pour more of his wisdom and understanding into me. Remember, God will send a word.

27

Don't Doubt and Expect It to Work Out

*Casting down arguments and every high thing that
exalts itself against the knowledge of God, bringing
every thought into captivity to the obedience of Christ.
(2 Corinthians 10:5 NKJV)*

The battle begins in the mind. I will keep this message simple. It is one of the toughest things to overcome without the proper knowledge.

I've pondered God's words to me many times. Often, he has shared a word with me that I did not expect to hear.

I used to doubt what He said to me. My immediate reaction was, "God, I don't believe that." Without hesitation, I would block his words with my doubt.

One day, my actions became clear to me. This happened as I realized that although many of my blessings were coming through despite my doubt, I was damaging myself by having the thoughts of doubt to begin with. Imagine how much I missed because I did not believe. I was dealing with more anxiety than I had ever had all because I allowed doubt to stand in the way. So I made an adjustment. As soon as God gave me a word, I would say, "Thank you, Jesus!"

28

What Are Your Priorities?

But seek first his kingdom and his righteousness, and
all these things will be given to you as well.
(Matthew 6:33 NIV)

I thank God for causing me to grow as a woman. In life, God is always working on our behalves, in ways that we do not expect.

One of the greatest things God taught me was about priorities. I was trying to understand why God gave me everything I wanted and sometimes wrapped the package in a way that was not initially appealing to me. I was looking by the standards of the world, although I had already put them aside for God's blessings.

As I was praying, I had to ask myself, *What are my priorities? Money, cars, clothes, accolades? Only to realize that God can give and take all of these things.* I was shocked yet humbled that God convicted me on how I was prioritizing my life.

You must be wondering what this is about. It's about wanting to be in a relationship but wanting that person to fulfill me in ways that were not realistic. I wanted to become a better and healthier person in life so that I might fulfill God's purpose and uphold his kingdom. I was looking for a man to bring to the table money, cars, clothes, degrees, and accolades. Although nothing is wrong with these things, more important matters need to be addressed when seeking someone.

God helped me understand what my priorities should be. Did this person bring happiness, peace, healthy emotions, the Word of God in its truth, self-control, and understanding? Did this individual pray with me? Was this person patient with me? Did this individual listen to me?

I'm not saying that this person should have made me happy. This individual should have been happy within, and I should have been before the two of us came together. This is not about perfection. This person would not be my everything but would listen and would be humble before the Lord to help me. I would still depend solely on the Lord to be my provider, protector, professor, confidant, comforter, peace, and everything. We would simply carry out God's purpose together.

Relationships are not about your life and what is pleasing to you, but they are about God himself. What are you doing to be beneficial in your relationship with others? Are you seeking individuals to be friends with just because they have connections to people with status, money, the most followers, information, etc.? Are these relationships for personal gain?

God taught me a great thing about perspective and the reason he positions us where we are in life so that we have the advantage. It's not so that we will misuse people but so that we will see what is being handed to us and the spirit it comes with. Having God's perspective allows us to decide whom we let into our lives and whom we let out. Not every deal seems so sweet. We can see right through a person's intentions. A person can also have the right intentions but the wrong spirit.

What am I saying? What are your priorities?

29

The Power of Retreating

*But Jesus often withdrew to lonely places
and prayed. (Luke 5:16 NIV)*

Thank you, Jesus, for being an example of how we ought to live and obey. When I retreated, I was able to hear God clearly and to see what he needed from me. At some point in time, life can become overwhelming for us all. But I thank God for the opportunity to pull away.

The power in retreating is that you can calm your mind and silence the noise. Clear away the distractions. This world has provided us with so many things that pull our attention in different directions, all at one time. Besides all the technology, we also have family, friends, and coworkers pulling on us. I urge you to take some time for yourself and breathe. Ask God to make a way for you to be still in the midst of the chaos. I know your job doesn't stop, and the dishes will continue to pile as high as your clothes bin. The grass needs to be cut. You have to cook dinner for ten. But God will make a way.

The power in retreating is that not only will you come back healthier and stronger, but God will also give you the wisdom and the knowledge to handle it all better than you would have before because he is just that good. He loves you that much. He said he would never leave you or forsake you.

Do you have a major project, a homework assignment, or a business venture you need to tackle, but the answers just aren't manifesting? You need to retreat. When I did so, amazing plans were laid out before me, book titles were revealed to me, and understanding and clarity about my family was placed in me. Not everything that I was trying to figure out in the midst of the chaos could be received until I found the power to retreat.

30

Coming Off Life Support

His mother said to the servants, "Do whatever he tells you." (John 2:5 NIV)

At some point in time, we must trust God to do what he says he is going to do. We must know that he created us to be mightier and stronger than the adversity we face daily. We must understand that in the beginning, he created us to have dominion over the earth.

On this journey, I learned to be bold before the Lord and to have faith in what he had given me. I learned that he said he would never leave me or forsake me. I remembered that I was made in his image and that he had given me air so that I could breathe.

We are more than conquerors. We are loved. We are wonderfully and fearfully made. We are healers. We are chain breakers, navigators, light bearers, royalty, truth speakers, and liberators. We are made in his image.

In John 14:12, Jesus said, "Very truly, I tell you, whoever believes in me will do the works I have been doing, and they will do even greater things than these, because I am going to the Father" (NIV). I encourage you to come off life support and do the work of the Father. He has much in store for you to see and achieve. He has many lives to heal and to raise from the dead.

31

Break the Cycle

*When Jesus saw him lying there, and knew that he
already had been in that condition a long time, He
said to him, "Do you want to be made well?" The sick
man answered Him, "Sir, I have no man to put me into
the pool when the water is stirred up; but while I am
coming, another steps down before me." Jesus said to him,
"Rise, take up your bed and walk." And immediately the
man was made well, took up his bed, and walked.*
(John 5: 6–9 NKJV)

We look for Jesus to perform miracles in ways that are familiar to and comfort us. I'm forever grateful that he wants to do more than that. I'm forever grateful that he knows a way of healing that we don't know so that only he can get all the praise and all of the glory.

In the previous scripture, the cycle was that every day for thirty-eight years, the man dealt with the same thing. He was looking to the wrong source for healing. But God showed up one day. Jesus already knew how long the man had been there and asked him one simple question: "Do you want to be made well?"

We all have a choice to make. At some point, we all deal with a cycle of some magnitude. In what area of your life have you been depending on the wrong source to heal you? How much longer will you wait?

I pray that as you have read this book, the Lord has blessed you tremendously. I pray that you have not heard the words of the vessel but the words of the Lord through his trusted vessel and faithful servant. I pray that God has spoken to you in many ways that you could not even fathom. I pray that you received the words in this book with a kind heart and calm mind.

I pray that God gives you clarity and peace that surpasses all understanding. I pray that God will expand your territory and reveal who you are in Christ. I pray that you no longer shrink back in the face of adversity but run at full speed the race that has been given to you.

I know God will never leave you or forsake you. I know God has not created you for such a time as this to be stuck or wondering if he will show up again. You know he is real. I know he is real. Break the cycle of doubt, confusion, mistrust, unforgiveness, procrastination and unworthiness. Let go of anything that is blocking you from your miracle.

Look to the right source. When he asks you, "Do you want to be made well?" you don't have to tell the Lord whom you've been looking to for healing. He is your redeemer. He already knows where you've been looking. He also knows that you are ready to break the cycle.

Are you ready?

Healing

Lord, I say thank you
For not throwing away my brokenness and
Thank you for the strength to
Stand firm in your word,
As I reach out into your vastness
Where you've held these pieces
Of me, waiting
For me to come back to you.
Empty and all
So that I may pull these broken pieces
Back into me
Until I am made whole again.
I thank you.

There is a
Balm in Gilead named Jesus Christ
Who will bind me back together with your glory and love.

Lord, I thank you
For allowing me to dine at your table of grace as you
Feed me your words of
Healing, understanding, wisdom, love, holiness, grace, mercy,
life, beauty, and confidence—

Everything that is you.

Lord, I thank you
That your word has
Released me
From all that was sent to destroy me.

Lord, I thank you
For your word and the fullness thereof.

Lord, I say thank you
For not throwing away my brokenness.
In Jesus's name, amen!

—Kendramiah P.

Printed in the United States
By Bookmasters